A GENOCIDE ALPHABET

TRANSMISSION

Transmission denotes the transfer of information, objects or forces from one place to another, from one person to another. Transmission implies urgency, even emergency: a line humming, an alarm sounding, a messenger bearing news. Through Transmission interventions are supported, and opinions overturned. Transmission republishes classic works in philosophy, as it publishes works that re-examine classical philosophical thought. Transmission is the name for what takes place.

A GENOCIDE ALPHABET

Toula Nicolacopoulos
George Vassilacopoulos

re.press

http://www.re-press.org
© authors and re.press 2025
The moral rights of the authors have been asserted

This work is 'Open Access', published under a creative commons license which means that you are free to copy, distribute, display, and perform the work as long as you clearly attribute the work to the authors, that you do not use this work for any commercial gain in any form whatsoever and that you in no way alter, transform or build on the work outside of its use in normal academic scholarship without express permission of the author (or their executors) *and* the publisher of this volume. For any reuse or distribution, you must make clear to others the license terms of this work. For more information see the details of the creative commons licence at this website: http://creativecommons.org/licenses/by-nc-sa/3.0/

IBSN: 978-1-7642346-1-0

Absolute crime

"Crime is the infinite judgement whereby right is infringed as right and what is mine is assailed, negated in such a way that if I were to allow it to happen, I should lose not only what belongs to me but in general that capacity for ownership" (Hegel)

Perfect crime

"The unjust man must […] if he is to be thoroughly unjust, be able to avoid detection in his wrongdoing; for the man who is found out must be reckoned a poor specimen, and the most accomplished form of injustice is to be seen just when you are not. So, our perfectly unjust man must be perfect in his wickedness; he must be able to commit the greatest crimes perfectly and at the same time get himself a reputation for the highest probity" (Plato)

European settler colonialism revolves around...

…committing the absolute crime and perfecting it

The absolute crime involves...

…criminal willing and criminal being

Perfecting the absolute crime involves...

...supremacist thinking

Criminal being and criminal willing involve...

…willing one's being *into being* by willing the other's being *out of being*

Supremacist thinking involves...

…presenting the agents of criminal being as builders of a just world by treating the other as less-than-a person / more-than-a thing

Criminal being is the compass of western European racist thinking

The western European coloniser is the cogito (I think, I am) of misology (hatred of truth) and misanthropy (hatred of the other's sovereign being)

The principle of the western European cogito is...

…I am (as criminal), I think (as racist)

The western European cogito
makes sense of being as exclusively
proprietary...

...I think myself as a person by willing my being into being as the owner of things

Western European proprietary cogito involves...

...the orientations of personhood and thinghood

So, 'I think myself as a person by willing my being into being as the owner of things' means...

…I think and will personhood and thinghood into proprietary being

'I think and will personhood and thinghood into proprietary being' involves...

…owning things and respecting persons

Owning things and respecting persons involves...

...treating personhood and thinghood as universal orientations

As universal orientations personhood and thinghood...

…define the capacity of universal humanity to own

In enacting the capacity to own, the western European cogito is...

...the pure (unmediated) will to own

The pure will to own involves...

…splitting/liberating personhood and thinghood from the integrative powers of authoritative traditions like the Greek, Christian, and Roman, and

…reintegrating personhood and thinghood as proprietary being

Western European pure willing involves...

...the universal principle, 'everything can be owned except for the capacity of persons to own'

'Western European willing/being is supremacist' means...

…the particularized (white) collective is constituted as the dominant Cogito (we think, we are)

The white supremacist collective Cogito...

...acts as the guardian of the capacity to own and as the exclusive creator and distributor of proprietary being

The western European proprietary cogito (willing being into being/willing the other's being out of being) is contradictory...

...its thinking and being of universal personhood and thinghood are split and held together by a self-privileging willing

'We think universals, we are the universal' means...

...the white supremacist collective Cogito suffers from the disorder of willing into being (colorless) universals (personhood/thinghood) through its exclusionary power over the capacity to be a person/owner

'To be in a state of disorder' means...

…to be emptying the universal orientations (personhood, thinghood) of their universality

'Emptying personhood and thinghood of their universality' means...

…simultaneously affirming and canceling them as universals

As universal orientations personhood and thinghood...

…orient the proprietary being of western Europeans everywhere in nature

As universals devoid of universality, personhood and thinghood...

...orient western Europeans in colonizing every place, pretending to spread universal humanity

Wherever it goes, (and in principle it thinks of itself as legitimately being everywhere before it arrives somewhere), the colonizing white supremacist Cogito...

…posits itself as the global creator, manager, and distributer of proprietary being

…wills itself into proprietary being by willing the other's being out of their being

…becomes the predator of being, of spirits, and of labour

As predator of being, the white supremacist Cogito claims...

...exclusive ownership of the capacity to own before claiming ownership of lands

As predator of being, spirits, and labour, it practices...

…ontological, spiritual, and economic violence against humanity, and it *is* this violence

The colonizing imperative of the white supremacist Cogito is...

...'Become the owners of foreign lands by willing your proprietary being into being, acting and thinking as if the lands were empty of owners'

Enacting the colonizing imperative of the white supremacist Cogito is...

…committing and perfecting the absolute crime

'Become the owners of foreign lands by willing your proprietary being into being acting and thinking as if the lands were empty of owners' means that...

...willing the other's being out of being (absolute crime) frames the practice of willing one's being into being

For the white supremacist criminality frames racism in that...

...ontological racism is grounded in the ontopathological disorder of proprietary being

The colonizing imperative of whiteness produces the ontopathological disorder of white supremacy...

...by enacting proprietary being hypothetically, *'as if'* criminal willing had not rendered its being null and void

White supremacy fills its void with…

…racist thinking that exorcises the criminality of *willing the other's being out of being*

This misology of racist thinking
(seeking to perfect the crime)...

…accompanies the misanthropy
of criminal willing and being
(committing the absolute crime)

The white supremacist orientations of misanthropy (criminal being) and misology (racist thinking) are one-dimensional, meaning...

...the white supremacist cogito prioritises their particular willing at the expense of universal thinking and being

As driven by criminal being, racism is on a mission to conceal the depth of the absolute crime by...

…presenting criminality as a just civilizational thinking and acting

Presenting criminality as a just civilizational thinking and acting involves...

…(mis)representing the other as
less-than-a-person / more-than-a-thing

As the product of willing the split between thinghood and personhood, that of the ontological and the ethical, criminal being produces the void of settler colonialisim onto (   ) ethics

We are (as criminals), we think (as racists)

onto (occupation / slave labour / ethnic cleansing / genocide) ethics

In the split between the ethical and
the ontological...

…the criminal void of settler colonialism encounters the resistance of sovereign being

Resistance means...

...racist thinking cannot perfect
(conceal as just) the absolute crime

Resistance exposes…

...white supremacist proprietary being as hypothetical (as null and void)

Resistance involves the commands...

…'you are the criminal, account for youself'

…'think with your (criminal) being as fully exposed to our (sovereign) being'

Receiving the commands (of sovereign being) means...

…bearing the full weight of the colonizer's world, by surrendering one's (misanthropic) being, and

…becoming a gatherer of the white supremacist collective's criminal histories, by giving up one's (misologist) thinking

Becoming the willing and alert gatherer of the white supremacist criminal histories requires...

…a new collective Cogito that invokes a mutually informing three-dimensional universality of being, thinking, and willing

A three-dimensional collective Cogito is capable of...

…re-thinking the universal orientations of personhood and thinghood (philosophically) and

…re-telling the story of the absolute crime and its failed perfection (historically)

Decolonizing involves...

...refering racist thinking back to its source in criminal willing and criminal proprietary being

www.ingramcontent.com/pod-product-compliance
Lightning Source LLC
Chambersburg PA
CBHW030908170426
43193CB00009BA/772